Learning Objectives For:

TELEPHONE SKILLS FROM A TO Z

The objectives for *Telephone Skills from A to Z, Revised Edition,* are listed below. They have been developed to guide you, the reader, to the core issues covered in this book.

THE OBJECTIVES OF THIS BOOK ARE:

❑ 1) To present basic telephone courtesies.

❑ 2) To show how to handle telephone conversation problems.

❑ 3) To explain what to avoid in telephoning.

ASSESSING YOUR PROGRESS

In addition to the learning objectives, Crisp Learning has developed an **assessment** that covers the fundamental information presented in this book. A twenty-five item, multiple choice/true-false questionnaire allows the reader to evaluate his or her comprehension of the subject matter. An answer sheet with a chart matching the questions to the listed objectives is also available. To learn how to obtain a copy of this assessment please call: **1-800-442-7477** and ask to speak with a Customer Service Representative.

Assessments should not be used in any selection process.

About The Author

Nancy Friedman, the Telephone Doctor®, has been setting the standards on telephone skills and customer service for thousands of corporations in the United States and abroad since 1983. Telephone Doctor® videos are available in seven languages and in 27 countries.

Nancy is regarded as "America's foremost and most sought-after speaker on customer service and telephone skills." She and her husband, Dick, work together at their Telephone Doctor® headquarters building in St. Louis, Missouri.

Nancy can be reached at:

The Telephone Doctor®
30 Hollenberg Court
St. Louis, MO 63044

Phone: 314-291-1012

Fax: 314-291-3710

email: Nancy@telephonedoctor.com
website: www.telephonedoctor.com

Telephone Skills from A to Z

The Telephone Doctor ® Phone Book

Revised Edition

Nancy J. Friedman
The Telephone Doctor®

A Fifty-Minute™ Book

CRISP LEARNING
Menlo Park, California

Telephone Skills from A to Z

The Telephone Doctor ® Phone Book

Revised Edition

Nancy J. Friedman

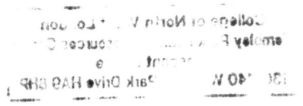

Credits:

Senior Editor: **Debbie Woodbury**
Copy Editor: **Charlotte Bosarge**
Production Manager: **Judy Petry**
Design: **Amy Shayne**
Production Artist: **Carol Lindahl**
Cartoonist: **Ralph Mapson**

© 1995, 2000 Crisp Publications, Inc.
Printed in the United States of America by Von Hoffmann Graphics, Inc.

Telephone Doctor® and Business Friendly® are registered servicemarks of The Telephone Doctor®, Inc.

CrispLearning.com

00 01 02 03   10 9 8 7 6 5 4 3 2 1

Library of Congress Catalog Card Number 00-101085
Friedman, Nancy J.
Telephone Skills from A to Z
ISBN 1-56052-580-0

This book is printed on recyclable paper with soy ink.

Dedication

This book is dedicated to several people. First, to my husband, Dick Friedman, for his constant support, love and understanding. And to my children, David and Linda, and their spouses, Robyn Friedman and Les Steinberg. Their humor lends significant insight.

To the entire Telephone Doctor® and Weatherline® staff who live Telephone Doctor® techniques daily, illustrating how easy it is to follow them.

To Esther and Arthur Mollner, my parents, and Gerry Mollner, my brother, all now deceased, whose guidance, love and encouragement made me what I am today. A special mention to Ed Pollock for his unfailing dedication to and support of this project. To Charlie Kopetzky, whose untimely death was a loss to all who knew him. Charlie wanted me to write this book eons ago using the title *Are You Able to Hold?*

Preface

This revised edition of *Telephone Skills from A to Z* includes the important topics of cell phones, email, online customer service and much more information on the ongoing saga of voicemail. Despite the development of electronic technology, how to be nice to people—what to say to them to make them feel good and make them want to come back—has not changed very much. It doesn't matter to Telephone Doctor® if you use two cans and a string to communicate with your customers. You can use the phone, email, fax, voicemail, "snail" mail, or work face-to-face with your customers—it is *what* and *how* you say things that matters to us. Speaking of email and fax, those methods need as much, if not more, attention due to the fact that more often than not the written word can be misinterpreted. With email and fax, you don't hear the voice and you especially aren't able to hear the smile. Pay close attention to those new sections if that is how you communicate most often with your customers.

Let's face it: Customer service is not rocket science. It is not brain surgery. We're not trying to cure cancer. We're just trying to be nice in dealing with our customers. Don't make it more difficult than it is. It's common sense, and, unfortunately, not practiced enough (as we all know). To get the most out of this book, we recommend you underline or highlight those skills and techniques you want to use later.

We have taken the most important skills, tips, ideas, and techniques for excellent telephone customer service and combined them all in this book. Electronic technology is here and will continue to change, but the all-important people skills—the contents of this book—are timeless. Being friendly to the caller *before* you know who it is will never go out of style. We remind you: most customer service *starts* on the phone.

So enjoy, and remember the Telephone Doctor® motto:

"It's Fun to Be Good!"

Nancy

Nancy J. Friedman

Contents

x

 Introduction

"Your people stink!"

With those succinct words, Telephone Doctor® history was born.

Early in 1983, I called my insurance agent after being treated rudely by his staff. I told him, "Your people stink!" He asked me what happened and I told him. "Your people are so rude, so abrupt, so unfriendly, so unhelpful–I don't want to do business with you anymore!" I told him that we treat our wrong numbers better than he treated his customers.

He understood. "You know, Nancy, you're right. When I call your office, I'm treated like a king, and I'm not even a customer."

Then he asked me to come over and show his staff what we did at our office.

I went to the agent's office and stood up in front of 10 to 12 people around a table–their pens and paper ready for some scientific strategy on how to be nice on the phone. Would you believe, when I told them at our office, we say, "Thank you" and "Please," they stopped to write down those words? That's right. They thought "thank you" and "please" were good ideas!

I spoke with them for about 20 minutes and when I was leaving, the president of the agency stopped me and told me "Thank you, we really learned some new things!" Dazed, I came home to my husband, Dick, and shared the story with him. "The president of the insurance agency told me that he really learned some new things," I said. "I don't understand." Dick told me, "Don't be surprised, Nancy. Nobody's ever shown them."

I mentioned this story to the general manager of a newspaper in Davenport, Iowa. The next day, he called me and asked me to come up to his newspaper and train his people. He said, "If there's a telephone on anyone's desk, he or she should be trained!" I wrote a half-day program, flew up to Davenport, and delivered the program four times. The first was to management only, because, as the general manager said: "If this program is to work, and I want it to, it must start at the top. It must dribble down. It can not dribble up."

After this first program, the paper's editor came up and told me, "Nancy, that was fabulous. You're very good. You sure have all the cures, don't you?" And he snapped his fingers, pointed at me, and said, "You're the doctor...you're the Telephone Doctor."

I told my husband that I had been dubbed the Telephone Doctor. "What do you think?" I asked. He replied, "I think we should get the name registered, because we're going to have some fun!"

And fun we've been having, traveling the world and training organizations to do a better job when the public calls.

Attitude: It's Your Choice

You have little or no control over many things in life, but you do have control over one essential quality: your attitude. Disinterested, bored, unmotivated people aren't very productive, and they achieve little satisfaction in life. In contrast, people who make an effort to have a positive and cheerful attitude typically reach many of their goals, and they usually are happier and more fulfilled!

Successful people normally have made two decisions about their attitude:

1. **I can control my attitude!** A cheerful and positive attitude can be created with practice and hard work. First of all, it requires belief in the fact that a positive attitude determines the quality of your life as much as any other single factor. Controlling your attitude demands dedication and a commitment to creating and maintaining this attitude.

2. **I will make the workplace an ideal site for my cheerful, positive attitude!** You spend a good percentage of your life in the work environment. But each week has a total of 168 hours. If you work full-time, you're only at the office about 40 hours—that is less than 25% of your week. So we're not asking for an awful lot of time to be positive. How you perceive and function in your workplace is key to creating a cheerful, positive attitude in every facet of your life. Any job can be boring, or it can be exciting and fulfilling. Your attitude will make the difference. Take each task and do it well, one step at a time. With a positive attitude, work will become fun. And you'll feel good about it, and about yourself, your co-workers, and your company.

So, yes, attitude is a matter of choice. It can be controlled, and doing your job well can become the basis for a positive attitude in your personal life as well.

There is a wonderful saying:
"Once a job has first begun, never leave it till it's done.
Be the labor great or small, do it well or not at all."

If you're going to do something anyway,
you might as well do it with a smile and make it fun.

ATTITUDE: IT'S YOUR CHOICE

1. Why do you think it's important to have a cheerful, positive attitude?

_____

_____

2. Name two things you can do to improve your attitude toward your job.

_____

_____

3. When do you believe would be the best time to dedicate yourself to improving your attitude?

_____

_____

Be Friendly Before You Know Who It Is

SEE ALSO "SIX CARDINAL RULES OF CUSTOMER SERVICE"

Have you ever called a company and were treated in a fairly average manner? Then the person with whom you're speaking realizes you're a friend of the boss or someone other than an average customer, and he or she brightens up! Why discriminate? Every customer is a form of job insurance for you! If you are friendly *before* you know who it is, you are giving the same good service to everyone. That is the way it should be. Treat *every* caller as though he or she is special. Every call, and every caller, is unique.

Some people who answer phone calls treat people they know (and like) very pleasantly, but "ordinary" callers get ordinary treatment. Why can't calls be answered in a friendly way all the time? Why are some calls—personal ones, for instance—greeted with one attitude, and calls from customers with another?

"Well," they say, "some calls are more fun—when my friends call, for example. Business calls are, well, just business. It's not like it's a conversation or anything. I just want to be efficient."

Efficiency is a worthy goal, but you need not sound like a human answering machine! With so many of today's calls being answered electronically, it is more important than ever to show your personality on *every* call. Be friendly to every caller before you know who it is. In doing this, you will avoid discriminating between two types of callers in your mind: family and friends, who get friendliness; and customers, who get unfriendly "efficiency."

The person who first answers the phone is the company "greeter." This first encounter sets the mood for the call. Callers mirror how they are treated. If you are friendly, they tend to be friendly in return. If your attitude is cool, very likely they will reflect that coolness back. A good reception implies a good company; a poor reception, a poor company.

Remember, your callers *are* your friends—your business friends! Renew your enthusiasm often, and rededicate yourself to being Business Friendly®.

BE FRIENDLY BEFORE YOU KNOW WHO IT IS

1. Can you tell when someone you call is friendly before answering the phone?

   _____

   _____

2. In what way can efficiency interfere with friendliness on the phone?

   _____

   _____

3. Why are business callers your friends?

   _____

   _____

*B*uffer Words
SEE ALSO "THREE-PART GREETING"

Here are some sample buffer words:

"Good morning."

"Good afternoon."

"Thanks for calling."

"Happy holidays!"

You use these in person, don't you? When you go up to someone at a party, stick out your hand and say, "Nice to meet you," "Good to see you," or "Hi, my name is Leigh, what's yours?" Those are all buffer words that help warm the relationship. Why not do the same on every telephone call?

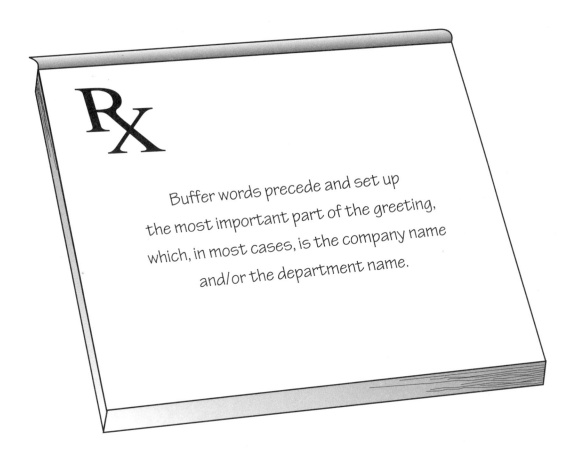

R_X

Buffer words precede and set up the most important part of the greeting, which, in most cases, is the company name and/or the department name.

*B*ureaucratic Bounce

Have you ever called a government office, organization, or association—any office with more than two floors—and had the following experience?

1. First, you get the operator (if you don't get the automated attendant):

   Operator: *"Hello, Acme Insurance."*

   You: *"Yes, I'd like to talk to someone about a change of address."*

   Operator: *"Address change? Oh. Well, I'm not sure. Hold on."*

2. Then:

   Next voice: *"Hello, may I help you?"*

   You: *"Yes, I'd like to change my address."*

   Next voice: *"Oh, well, I don't know how to do that. Hold on."*

3. Then:

   Third voice: *"Hello."*

   You: *"Yes, I'd like to talk to someone there about changing my address on your records. I'm not getting my mail."*

   Third voice: *"Well, I don't handle address changes. Let me see if I can find someone else. Hold on."*

4. Then:

   Operator: *"Hello."*

   You: *"Yes, can you help me have my address changed?"*

   Operator: *"Oh, it's you. Didn't anyone help you yet?"*

   You: *"No, that's why I'm still on the line."*

   Operator: *"Well, I'm not sure who can help you. But I think the lady you need to speak to is Mary Smith. And she's not in today. She should be in tomorrow. Try then, okay?"*
   Click!

The Bureaucratic Bounce (bouncing from one department to another without any help whatsoever) has to be one of the absolutely worst examples of ineffective telephone service! It happens all the time, and that is unfortunate—because the solution is simple: *job knowledge!*

Yes, job knowledge—knowing your job and knowing your company—is the cure for the Bureaucratic Bounce. No matter what your caller wants to know about your company, firm, or organization, your answer should be: "That's a good question. Let me check and find out." Because you *will* be able to find out if you try. You *can* get the information. It is your job, your responsibility, to help the caller once you answer the phone. If you don't know, find out. Help each and every caller get the information or service he or she needs.

When you answer the telephone on behalf of your company, you have accepted 100% responsibility for that telephone call. Job knowledge and training is the key. Know who the president of the company is, find out the names of the department heads and what they do, and be aware of your company's products and services.

Remember, with every phone call, you represent the company as well as yourself. Take full responsibility for the telephone call. If you aren't able to provide an answer, get a name and phone number so you or someone else can call the party back. Follow the advice of the Telephone Doctor®: Eliminate the Bureaucratic Bounce with a caring attitude and by knowing your job and your company.

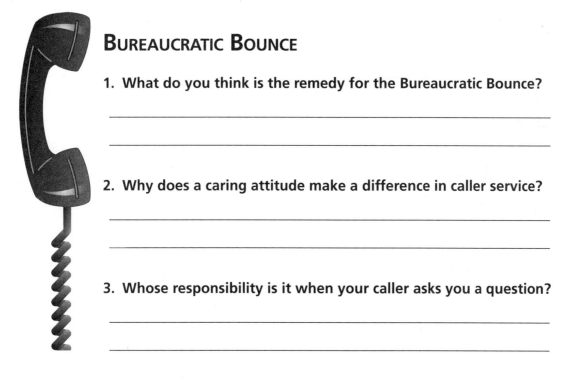

BUREAUCRATIC BOUNCE

1. **What do you think is the remedy for the Bureaucratic Bounce?**

   _____

   _____

2. **Why does a caring attitude make a difference in caller service?**

   _____

   _____

3. **Whose responsibility is it when your caller asks you a question?**

   _____

   _____

Call Centers

Formerly called Customer Service Departments, call centers are growing in number, popping up in virtually every industry. Call centers, by definition, are departments within an organization that are staffed by personnel normally called Customer Service Representatives, or CSRs, who take and/or make calls for a product or service.

Here are the Telephone Doctor®'s TEN BEST CUSTOMER SERVICE TECHNIQUES. By using even one of them, you are bound to see an increase in satisfied customers. So whether you are already the best or you need a re-fresher course, these techniques will be a welcome addition.

1. BE A DOUBLE CHECKER. Learn to use those exact words. Everyone loves it when you double check something for them. Even if you are pretty sure the item is out of stock or the appointment is filled, it sounds so good to hear, "Let me double check that for you." This particular phrase is a great stress-reducer for the customer. It also says, "You may be right, let me see." Double checking something offers that one more step of going the extra mile. You will find yourself getting thanked much more often when you double check something for your customers.

2. PRETEND IT'S YOU. If you're working with a customer, either on the phone or in person, and he or she needs something–pretend it's you. What would *you* want to have happen? What would make *you* happy? What would make *you* satisfied? Here is a great place to remember the Golden Rule: "Do unto others as you would have them do unto you." It is amazing to see people treating customers one way and then finding out that *they* would not want to be treated like that.

3. GET INVOLVED. Let customers know you are on their team. If you are ringing up a purchase for someone, mention how nice her choice is. If you are helping someone with a trip of some sort, get excited with him. When customers feel as though you are part of the package, they love it. Not mentioning anything tells the customer that you really do not care one way or the other. When you involve yourself with the customer's situation, things really go much more smoothly.

4. STAY FOCUSED. Eye contact is critical in delivering excellent customer service. Heads that turn on a spindle and look everywhere but at the customer get very few good marks in customer service. Eye contact shows you are listening. Even though eye contact is impossible on the phone, you can learn to stay focused. Do not type into a computer unless it pertains to what you are doing. Never read while you are on the phone with a customer. Stay focused on the caller even without eye contact. When you are not concentrating on what you are doing with the customer, mistakes can happen.

5. DO SOMETHING EXTRA. There is usually always something extra you can do for the customer. In most of the cases, it won't even cost very much, and customers love that something extra—oddly enough, even if they cannot use it. The thought of getting something free is very special to the customer. Even if you do not have anything tangible to "give away," the something extra can be just an extra "thank you" note, email, or call to the customer. Extra thank you's are always appreciated.

6. SHOW YOUR TEETH. In Telephone Doctor® language, that means to smile. There are many people who think they are smiling, but aren't. So Telephone Doctor®'s motto is: "Show Your Teeth." Smiling is one of the best customer service techniques there is. It is frustrating to walk into a store, or call some place, and not see or hear a smile. (And, yes, you can hear a smile!) Remember, if your teeth are not showing, you are not smiling!

7. ASK QUESTIONS. A super way to offer superior customer service is to ask questions. Build on what the customer is talking about. Listen for one or two words that you can ask something about. Even a simple "Tell me more," will work. Once customers are talking, you will be better able to help them. Asking questions tells the customer, "You are special, and I want to help you."

8. USE COMPLETE SENTENCES. One-word answers are semi-useless in customer service. And one-word answers are definitely perceived as rude. "Yes," "no," and the like tell the customer, "I am not really interested in you or what you need." It is important to remember that when you work on a phone, nodding *is not* an answer. The customer *needs* to hear you speak.

9. CARE. Most people have what the Telephone Doctor® calls the *care gene*. Some people use it more than others; others forget they have it. Learn to care what your customers' needs are and they will take care of you.

10. LAUGH. Laughter will always lighten the load. Everyone likes to laugh. Take the time to laugh and enjoy your customers.

Put any one or any combination of these Telephone Doctor® customer service tips into action and watch what happens. Each can make customer service special. Each will result in happier customers. And a happier *you*.

Cellular Phones

In today's business environment cellular phones are everywhere. It is also hard to go anywhere in public without seeing someone talking on a cell phone–in a restaurant, on the street, on the bus, in a car. Unfortunately, the greater the number of cell phones, the greater the opportunity for these devices to intrude and interrupt others' privacy.

Many public places have banned cell phones from being used. Movie theaters and restaurants in particular are asking that patrons turn their cell phones or ringers off. Use of cell phones by drivers of passenger vehicles has even been addressed in recent legislation, as many states attempt to pass laws prohibiting cell phone use while driving.

Proper cell phone etiquette

The following are guidelines for cell phone use. Remember, most of these apply to use of car phones as well, since most people now use a single device for both locations:

➤ **When you make a cell phone call, always notify the *first* person you speak with that you are on a cell phone.** This lets the called party know that if the connection should be lost (and it often is), you have not hung up on them. This is polite, but it also has the added effect of making your call more urgent and often speeds the connection to the called party.

➤ **Please, *never* use a cell phone at a table in a restaurant.** If you must have your phone with you, explain to the caller that you are in a restaurant, then take the call away to a place that is less disruptive, or, better, offer to call the person back. No one wants to hear your conversation–it is uncomfortable for those at your table and an annoyance for the other diners. You only need to turn the phone back on should you need it for an emergency, or if you need to make a call to the office to remind them of something.

➤ **If you are in a meeting or at a conference, always turn your cell phone off.** There is almost nothing ruder that getting–and taking–a call in the middle of an important presentation or conversation.

➤ **Make sure you have a back-up message service or voicemail** for when you get disconnected, your battery gets low, or you need to turn your phone off. That way people will not be frustrated because they cannot reach you.

➤ **When in public, avoid loud or animated conversations.** Avoid extended calls.

In a car

1. **Use the speed dialer, if possible.** Every time you take your eyes off the road to push one button, you take a chance. Focus on safety first.

2. **If you have a passenger that can dial for you, all the better.**

3. **While you're driving, never use the phone to make any kind of sales presentation or deep negotiations.** If you need to talk about something important, pull off the road, stop the car, and then have your conversation.

4. **Use of a hands-free or "cradle" speakerphone in the car is recommended.** It lets you keep both hands on the wheel, where they should be. If you are in an accident, insurance companies are now asking if you were on the phone while you were driving. It's senseless to try to get out of it, because the phone records can tell if you were or not.

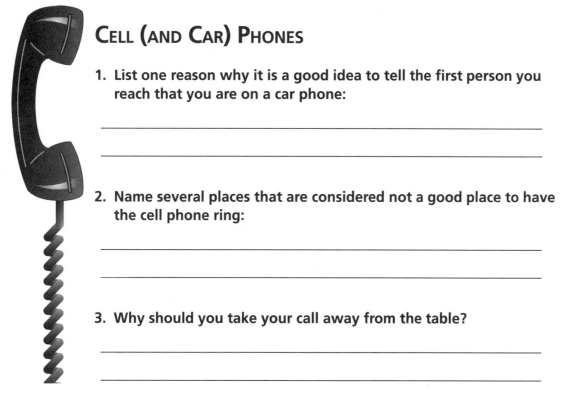

CELL (AND CAR) PHONES

1. List one reason why it is a good idea to tell the first person you reach that you are on a car phone:

    _____

    _____

2. Name several places that are considered not a good place to have the cell phone ring:

    _____

    _____

3. Why should you take your call away from the table?

    _____

    _____

Cliff-Hangers

Caller: "Mr. Jones, please."

Receptionist: "He's gone."

Caller: (without missing a beat)
"Oh? When did he die?"

Replies such as "He's gone," and other one- or two-word answers are called cliff-hangers. They just leave people hanging. Cliff-hangers can be disappointing and frustrating for your callers. They are also thought of as rude.

Try not to do that to any caller. Make complete statements. Do not just say, "She's not in," or "He's out to lunch." Have an additional backup statement ready.

It's so much more helpful to:

➤ Offer to take a message

➤ Offer to help

➤ Get someone else who can help

CLIFF-HANGERS

1. List two cliff-hangers you have been the recipient of:

_____

_____

2. List two cliff-hangers you have used:

_____

_____

3. For a cliff-hanger that you have used, rewrite it below to be more helpful to the caller:

_____

_____

Company Jargon

SEE ALSO "SIX CARDINAL RULES OF CUSTOMER SERVICE"

Simply put, company jargon should stay within your company. Using it with outside callers often causes mistakes and miscommunications. You are far more familiar with these terms and abbreviations than the caller, and you will not impress anyone with words or technical knowledge they don't understand. Just the opposite—you will annoy them. To maximize communication and understanding, use common English without "alphabet soup" abbreviations.

Avoid jargon; speak on the caller's level.
Do not use "military" language on "civilians."

Controlling the Conversation

Callers sometimes shift from topic to topic, or they get carried away on a subject that has no connection to your business or why they called. This may be okay when you have some time and are trying to build rapport on the telephone. However, you usually won't have time for a wandering discussion. Other calls may be coming in, or an important task may require your immediate attention.

What you need to do in this case is *take control of the conversation*. The recommended Telephone Doctor® technique is called "Back-on-Track."

For example, you ask: *"And when do you want us to deliver the bike? We can schedule a delivery Wednesday morning or Friday afternoon."*

Customer: *"Well, let's see now. I have an uncle coming in from out of town. He's quite a guy. He's a professional fishing guide. His specialty is shark fishing. He was telling us the other day that he landed an 800-pound great white shark. We'll, that's not the world record, I guess, but it took a three-hour battle to land it. Ever go deep-sea fishing?"*

"Back-on-Track" response: *"I haven't, and that would be a good reason to have the bike delivered early, wouldn't it? You may even want to ride it before your uncle comes in. Now, would you like to get the bike on Wednesday morning or Friday afternoon?"*

See what happened? By listening, you took control of the conversation by *asking a question*—a related question—that steered the caller back-on-track and redirected the conversation.

If you are not able to think of a related question, try this more direct approach:

You: *"Well, that's very interesting, but I know you called to arrange your bike delivery and I want to be able to help you. Which day would you like the bike delivered—Wednesday or Friday?"*

Taking control of the conversation enables you to serve the caller and keep the conversation from wandering, so you don't spend any more time on the call than absolutely necessary.

Often the most effective route to serving your callers is to help them express what they want and guide them to make a decision. You assist them in getting to the point, so that you can help them. In other words, you serve them by managing and controlling the phone call!

CONTROLLING THE CONVERSATION

1. What should you do with "wandering" discussions?

_____

_____

2. What's the value of the Back-on-Track response?

_____

_____

3. What's the one ingredient necessary when controlling the conversation?

_____

_____

Don't Be Too Busy to Be Nice

SEE ALSO "SIX CARDINAL RULES OF CUSTOMER SERVICE"

Always be nice, no matter how busy you are. Being busy does not make it acceptable to sound rushed, harried, or rude—everyone is busy at one time or another. When someone asks you how things are going, a simple: "Great! How can I help you?" is always appropriate, then move the conversation along. If you complain about being too busy, you may scare your caller away. Customers want and deserve all of your attention. If you appear too busy, they may go elsewhere.

TRUE TELEPHONE TALES

Randy, the owner of a small advertising agency, made it a policy to greet his customers on the phone himself, enthusiastically and warmly, every time they called. One day he was extremely abrupt and curt to a regular customer, Jo, and she asked if everything was okay. "You're usually so nice," she said. He cut her off to say, "Jo, I'm too busy to be nice today."

Jo did not call back, and Randy eventually went out of business.

DEF 3 *E*ight Great Hates

Several years ago, Telephone Doctor® did a survey with *USA Today* to find out what bugs you on the telephone. "Being put on hold" was the winner. However, there were seven other frustrating events on the telephone. Here are the Eight Great Hates:

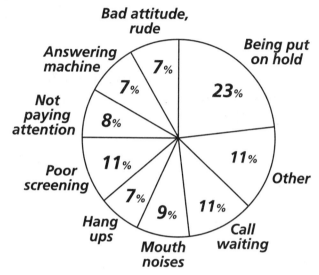

Did you notice voicemail was not even on the list? That survey was taken a while back. The more recent survey did put voicemail in the list of Eight Great Hates, but not where you might think: Voicemail was number two on the list. Guess what was number one the second time we did the survey? *Being put on hold* remained the number-one frustration of the American public.

EIGHT GREAT HATES

1. **What is your personal "great hate" in telephone calls?**

   _____

   _____

2. **Name three things you can do to eliminate the great hates.**

   _____

   _____

Email

We have said, "Voicemail—Curse or Cure?" Now we may wonder that about email, too. While certainly a marvel of communication, email can be a big frustration. But remember, it is just one more method of communicating with your customer.

Email's biggest problem

The largest single problem most people have with email is that it is too easy for one message to go inadvertently to an entire group when you only intended it to go to a single person. The result can be jobs lost, relationships shattered, and embarrassment on a grand scale.

However, even if it goes to only one person, your message can effortlessly be forwarded to someone else, who can forward it to someone else, and so on. You are better off not putting *anything* in an email that you wouldn't want in tomorrow's newspaper.

Jokes on email

For the most part this will depend on the email policy of your company. You should ask about it before any jokes come to you or you send any out. Email abuse is a large concern for many corporations and employees have been fired for violating company email policies. Some organizations already have software in place to alert management about inappropriate email content, inbound and outbound, and companies usually have the right to read employees' email without their consent.

You should also be aware that some computer networks will archive old messages even if you think you have deleted them. Email is a terrific way to communicate with customers and friends but it can be abused and eat up productive time on non-business matters. Find out what your company's policy on receiving personal email is: Know it and observe it.

Confidential matters on email

Personal email on business time can and should be avoided. Always be aware that what you write could be viewed by many, many people with just the touch of one button. You're better off keeping your personal correspondence confidential and separate from your business matters.

Sending angry emails

You have heard of irate callers, right? Well, now there are irate emails. If you are about to send an angry email: Stop. It might be wise to put your thoughts down on paper first, then reread what you wrote and take a cooling off period (overnight if need be) *before* replying. Cooling off first will help you decide if an angry email is the best way to accomplish your goal.

Unanswered emails

When people are asked what they think about people who do not return phone calls, the answer usually is, "Not very much." The same can be said about people who do not return emails. If your company uses email to communicate with customers, be ultra-responsive. Rapid response is looked at as excellent customer service. You may have heard horror stories about companies that take days—sometimes weeks—answering a simple request from a customer on email. As with not returning phone calls, not responding to emails is considered rude and definitely regarded as poor customer service.

Hiding behind email

Some people are accused of hiding behind their voicemail and being selective about returning calls. Recent surveys show that workers in the U.S. admit using email this way—specifically to avoid speaking with people in person. (Survey conducted by CommCore Consulting, the Electronic Messaging Assn., and the *Council on Communication Management-Training and Development Magazine,* 12/99).

EMAIL

1. What is one of the biggest complaints about email?

   _____

   _____

2. What is a major reason for customers abandoning their ecommerce shopping carts without completing the transaction?

   _____

   _____

Emotional Leakage

"Emotional leakage" in simple terms is getting angry at Peter and taking it out on Paul. In customer service, it is important not to let an earlier negative experience affect your dealings with an innocent caller—somebody who was not even involved. It is not right, it is not fun, it is not fair, and, of course, it is very rude. But it happens all the time, and often when you're not aware of it!

When something negative happens before that phone rings—you are alone in the office handling all the phones, the computer is down, your car ran out of gas this morning, or the last caller was angry and unreasonable—you need to remember that none of this is your current caller's fault.

It may be especially difficult to remember and accept this when you get several complaint calls in a row. Some days are like that. You can almost anticipate another hassle every time the phone rings. But don't let the caller hear that in your voice.

Curing emotional leakage is not that complicated, and these four steps will work for you:

1. **Let the phone ring one more time.** One more ring will not hurt, but answering the phone in an angry mood will. Use this moment to pause and relax.

2. **Take one or two deep breaths.** This is a proven calming influence, recommended by psychologists.

3. **Smile**—Let the smile show in your voice.

4. **Then answer the telephone.**

24

Successful telephone professionals handle
all situations with a positive attitude!
They put past annoyances aside,
and treat each call as a fresh experience.

EMOTIONAL LEAKAGE

1. Describe one time you experienced emotional leakage.

_____

_____

2. What's the key thought to remember about emotional leakage?

_____

_____

3. List the techniques you can use to combat emotional leakage.

_____

_____

Fast Talkers

Aggravating, aren't they? Fast talkers are frustrating; however, they can be handled.

Your first instinct may be to yell at the caller and say, "What do you think I am? A recording machine? I cannot write as fast as you talk!" But put those feelings on hold, and wait for the caller to take a breath—and he or she will. When you hear the pause, interject the following: *"Excuse me. I'm having a little difficulty understanding you. If you would please slow down just a bit, I'll be able to get this all correct for you."* It really works! That is what the caller wants: to be assured that you are going to get all the information.

Remember, you do not want to accuse anyone with words such as "Stop going so fast," or "I can't understand a thing you're saying." Those are not caller-friendly words and they will not be appreciated.

*F*ive Forbidden Phrases

The Five Forbidden Phrases were collected from scores of radio and television shows on which the Telephone Doctor® has appeared. Customers called in and talked about what they never wanted to hear on the telephone. Interestingly enough, from California to New York, from Texas to Minnesota, the same five things annoyed most people.

If you memorize the Five Forbidden Phrases and learn to avoid them, using the recommended responses instead, you will get immediate, positive results.

Forbidden Phrase	Recommended Response
1. "I don't know."	1. "Gee, that's a good question. Let me check and find out."
2. "Just a second."	2. "It may take me a few minutes to get that information. Are you able to hold while I check on that?"
3. "No" at the start of a sentence.	3. Eliminate it at the start of a sentence.
4. "We can't do that."	4. "That's a tough one. Let me see what I can do."
5. "You'll have to…"	5. "What you'll need to do…"

FIVE FORBIDDEN PHRASES

1. What is your choice for the most irritating forbidden phrase?

   _____

   _____

2. Name an additional phrase (to these five) that you wish were
   forbidden. Offer positive alternatives:

   _____

   _____

3. Suggest why the recommended responses are more effective:

   _____

   _____

Foreign Accents

Call it simple kindness or call it common sense, but learning to deal with language accents that are foreign to you can definitely be good for business. For many people, English is their second language. These people represent a sizable market for any corporation selling products or services in the United States. Or, perhaps English is *your* second language–in either case, from time to time the phone calls you answer may be from people whose accents are unfamiliar to you.

Here are five rules to remember when dealing with a foreign accent:

1. DO NOT PRETEND TO UNDERSTAND. If you do not understand the person you are speaking with, it is perfectly okay to say you are having difficulty understanding him or her. Ask the person to slow down, so you can get all the information correct. Hanging up without knowing what the caller wants is not good customer service!

2. DO NOT RUSH. Rushing threatens callers. Take the time–usually only a few seconds–to do it right. Listen to the caller's pattern of speech. You will be able to pick up key words. Repeat the key words back to clarify. Callers will appreciate the fact that you are really listening.

3. DO NOT SHOUT. People with accents are not hard of hearing and you don't need to repeat one word over and over to be sure they understand. Remember, people with an accent usually speak two languages, so it will take them a little longer to go through the thought processes: their native language for thinking, and English for communicating with you.

4. DO NOT BE RUDE. If you've ever told a caller, "I can't understand you," "Huh?" or even "What did you say?" you've been a little rude whether you intended to be or not. It is much better to stop, take full responsibility, and explain you are having difficulty understanding. Say, *"If you'll repeat it for me again, I'll be able to assist you."* It is a subtle difference, but a key one.

5. DO KEEP A JOB AID AVAILABLE. If most of the calls you receive are predominantly from one particular ethnic group, keep a handy job aid near your phone–a list with a few commonly-used phrases–to get you off the hook. For example, in Spanish "Un momento, por favor" means "One moment, please." Even if you pronounce it poorly it would be appreciated by a Latino who is having difficulty trying to communicate with you over the phone. You can then pause and bring someone to the phone who can help the customer.

Unknown

Making an effort to understand and respond to people with language accents is not just common courtesy, it's better business.

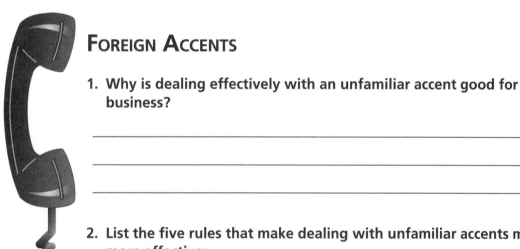

FOREIGN ACCENTS

1. **Why is dealing effectively with an unfamiliar accent good for business?**

   _____

   _____

   _____

2. **List the five rules that make dealing with unfamiliar accents much more effective:**

   _____

   _____

   _____

3. **How does a job aid help?**

   _____

   _____

   _____

Telephone Skills from A to Z

Front-Line Operators

SEE ALSO "RECEPTIONIST"

Front-line operators have one of the most harried, hurried, hassle-filled positions in any company. Not everyone can be a good operator. It takes dedication. Unfortunately, these unique, talented people are often underpaid and underappreciated.

As the company "greeter" and goodwill ambassador, the operator sends a signal of what the company is all about. This person helps set the mood for the rest of the call. That is why training in this position is vitally important.

TRUE TELEPHONE TALES

A personnel agency's client once asked how to find a good operator. At that time, his practice was to write an ad, place it in the newspaper, and use the post office box to avoid a lot of calls. The resumes were reviewed and then the applicants were scheduled for interview appointments. They would take a spelling test, a typing test, and a math test. When asked, "What about the voice test?" the client said, "What voice test?"

It is important to consider the voice qualities of the person who will be first to answer the calls that come into a business. When you are filling any position that requires heavy telephone usage, try to do the first interview by phone when possible!

FRONT-LINE OPERATORS

1. What is the value of the front-line operators?

_____

_____

2. Why is training important for operators?

_____

_____

3. Why should the first interview for an operator be made on the telephone?

_____

_____

Getting a Phone Number

Have you ever encountered this scene?

You: *"Fine, Mr. Smith. Please let me have your phone number and I'll see that she gets your message."*

Mr. Smith: *"Oh, she has it!"*

Ever hear that and then find that no one has the phone number? Want to have it never happen again? Well, you came to the right place. Use the "Easy Reference" technique when asking the caller for a phone number. It works like a charm.

Mr. Smith: *"Yes, please have her call me."*

You: *"I sure will, Mr. Smith. I know she probably has your phone number, but for 'easy reference,' would you run it by me one more time, please?"*

This technique works every time. In the unlikely event that the caller refuses, or insists, "I told you she has it!" and then hangs up, try the white pages, the yellow pages, your Rolodex, directory assistance, the computer, or anything else. But try to never deliver a message to anyone without a phone number.

GETTING A PHONE NUMBER

1. Why is it important to always get a phone number?

_____

_____

2. What is the value of the "Easy Reference" technique?

_____

_____

3. What can you do if the caller won't leave a number?

_____

_____

Gum Chewing

Chewing gum while talking to a customer—on the phone or in person—is simply not acceptable. End of subject!

Hold

Remember, being put on hold won first place in our Eight Great Hates survey. There are two reasons to put someone on hold.

You need to have the caller wait while you:

➤ Look for a person

➤ Look for information

Holding for a person

If the person to whom your caller wants to speak is on the phone or temporarily away, rather than keep the caller on hold, try to service the call immediately yourself. It sounds like this: *"Mr. Jones is on another call. I'm not sure how long he'll be. Let me have your name and number and I'll see that he gets your message."* (The second sentence is important. If you do not say it, the caller will respond, *"Well, how long do you think he'll be?"* This way, you address the objection *before* it is raised.) The third sentence is called the "Let Me" technique.

If you are in a position of strength (a secretary, assistant, or someone else who can help), use this Service Statement: *"My name is Kyle, I work with Mr. Jones. How can I help you? What can I do for you?"*

Either the Service Statement or the "Let Me" technique will get the ball rolling. Both the caller and the person being called will appreciate it. Everyone gets helped!

If you are in a front-line position and Mr. Jones is taking another call, using the "Let Me" technique as noted is always effective. Since most front-line employees do not have time to take long messages, this technique usually does the trick. It is better than asking, "Can I take a message?" which is weak and ineffective. Getting the name and phone number is preferred, and moves the call along much more quickly.

A woman had been working the front-line phones for quite a while. After attending a seminar, she marveled at what she had learned. "I've been saying 'Can I take a message?' for years—and been so rushed every time I said it—I came to never want to say it again. The "Let Me" technique is so much more effective and time-saving. I can't believe it took me this long to realize it!"

Even though most companies have voicemail, it is very important to offer the caller the option of leaving a personal message instead of one in a voicemail box. *Always* ask if you can offer the caller voicemail first; do not just dump the caller unceremoniously to the voicemail system.

By the way, if you do take a message, be sure to tell the caller, *"I'll be sure he/she gets your message."* Do not say "I'll be sure to have him/her call you." That is not your job. Your job is to ensure the message gets delivered to the called party.

Holding for information

Interestingly enough, most people don't mind holding for information as much as for a person. Why? Because most of the time the caller gets what he or she called for.

When someone is calling for information, the *Able* technique is best. Ask if the caller is "able to hold," give a visual clue of what you'll be doing to help while you are gone, and then wait for a response. You usually get immediate positive feedback. For example:

> **Caller:** *"I need to find out about my last payment."*
>
> **You:** *"Fine. If you're able to hold, I can get you that information, but I need to check the computer. Are you able to hold?"*

Then wait for a response. Callers greatly appreciate this technique.

Returning to a caller on hold

When you return to the phone, tell the caller, *"Thank you for holding"* first, then, *"I have the information you need."* It is only fair, after you have asked if they are able to hold, that you thank him or her for holding. You would be amazed how many people don't thank a caller for holding.

HOLD

1. Why is being put on hold so annoying?

_____

_____

2. List the two reasons for putting a caller on hold:

_____

_____

3. In holding for a person, what is the Service Statement, and why is it important?

_____

_____

4. Why is the "Able" technique key to successfully holding for information?

_____

_____

5. Upon returning to a caller on hold, what should you say?

_____

_____

38

"How Can I Help You?"

SEE ALSO "MESSAGE TAKING"

A reminder: This Service Statement is not recommended in the initial greeting. That's why you answered the phone. "How can I help you" is suggested for use for someone who has the time and ability to help the caller, or someone in a message-taking area.

"I Don't Know"

SEE ALSO "FIVE FORBIDDEN PHRASES"

There's no need to *ever* utter these three words. If you don't know the answer to a customer's question, *find out.* That's your job. There isn't a thing (outside of sensitive and financial information) that you can't find out if you try.

When you don't have information that's been requested, you can use this response instead: *"That's a good question. Let me check and find out. Are you able to hold?"* Then go find out.

*I*nternal Calls
SEE ALSO "WE ARE CUSTOMERS TO EACH OTHER"

All callers should be treated equally,
whether they are in-house personnel
or outside clients, customers, or consultants.
Answer your phone the same way every time,
whether it is an internal or external call.
You will be glad you did.

*I*nternet

When you think of customer service, you generally think of face-to-face and telephone interaction. However, due to the increasingly popularity of the Internet, electronic commerce (ecommerce) is becoming a growing area of customer service. As a result, consumer demand for immediate and complete customer service response is also growing. Often, even if a customer makes a purchase online, most still want the *option* of accessing a human being.

In theory, using the Internet and email to conduct business is ideal—there is no busy signal and no 30-minute "hold" time before reaching someone. It allows the customer to feel he or she has a special one-on-one relationship with the business and it allows the business to reach online audiences quickly and effectively. But there is problem with ecommerce: Surveys show that more than 60% of people that go online to purchase products *leave* their shopping cart and exit without buying anything because they cannot reach a human being to get immediate answers they need. As more people do business on the Internet, you will find you have more Internet-related service calls.

Reasons a customer may still need telephone service despite the Internet:

➤ The customer is uncomfortable with new technology and prefers to browse online, then use the phone to place the order.

➤ The customer is leery of entering personal and credit card information over the Internet and prefers to give the information over the telephone.

➤ The customer requires additional information on a product or service or is frustrated because he or she has questions that cannot be answered by the website.

➤ The customer is having technical problems while trying to place an order and needs to phone in for assistance and/or troubleshooting.

Most ecommerce sites make an effort to supply outstanding customer service to Internet customers. As a result, this treatment is becoming the high standard that the public expects both on the computer *and* on the phone. In years ahead, the companies that prosper will be the ones with great customer service—whether via Internet, phone, voicemail, fax, or in person. The Internet does not make telephone service obsolete; rather, it expands the role of the customer service representative.

As a telephone service professional, you must learn to think of the Internet and email as *part* of telephone service and continue to serve all your customers the same old-fashioned way you always have—promptly and politely.

Rx

Even though websites are designed to make it easy to interact with a company, buying or selling products and services on the Internet requires the same rapid response and attention to customer needs as communicating with the customer on the telephone.

*I*rate Callers

If your job entails taking calls from unhappy callers, you have your work cut out for you. You may be vulnerable to outbursts from dissatisfied customers or associates, or perhaps experiencing a disaster or other stressful situation. Handling this type of call takes time and training, but it *can* be accomplished effectively. Here are some techniques for turning unhappy callers into satisfied customers.

Get off on the right foot

Realize that an angry customer is not unhappy with you, but with the *situation*. Do not take the hostility personally. You are the lighting rod, not the target.

You can do a great deal to diffuse a caller's anger before you even pick up the phone. How? By *smiling* before you answer that call. A smile really can be heard in your voice over the phone. Your caller will find it more difficult to be rude to someone who is warm and friendly.

Use the ASAP technique

There are four basic steps to handling an irate caller. Together they are called the ASAP technique:

A pologize and Acknowledge the Caller's Feelings

You will probably spend about 80% of your time soothing the caller and about 20% actually working on the problem. Acknowledging feelings is the key to customer satisfaction: *"I'm sorry the information was incorrect. No wonder you're upset."*

S ympathize with the Caller. Empathize!

Put yourself in the caller's position; imagine how you would feel if you were calling with this same complaint or problem. You can show your interest in the situation by making statements such as, *"I don't blame you for being upset. That's got to be very frustrating."*

A ccept the Responsibility

Every time you answer the telephone on behalf of your company, you have accepted 100% responsibility for the call. You can say, *"Let me see how I can help. My name is Mary. I'm the customer service manager. And I'm speaking with…?"* Always introduce yourself, and if you have a title, now is the time to use it to create credibility. Re-introducing yourself will help speed the rapport-building process.

P repare to Help

Indicate that you sincerely care about the caller's problem. Be sure to use the caller's name—that usually helps to diffuse the anger. Once you have done this, begin to draw out what happened by asking questions. *"Thanks, Mr. Jones. Again my name is Mary. Let's see how I can help you."*

Don't make excuses

Don't make excuses to a complaining caller! No one wants to hear, "The computer is down," or "I'm the only one in the office." That is your problem, not the caller's. When you give an excuse, what the caller hears is, "I'm not going to help you now."

Avoid transferring the call

Sometimes you will not be able to solve the problem on the spot. Often you will need more information from another department, or the call may have to be handled by another person. Although these are legitimate courses of action, they will usually upset the caller again.

When you need more information, *tell* the caller that. Ask if he or she is able to hold while you obtain it, or if he or she would prefer to have you call back. Avoid using untrue phrases such as "Hold on a sec." *Nothing* takes a second.

If you need to transfer the caller, give the name of the person with whom he will be speaking. Explain why you are bringing in a third party. *"Joe, Mrs. Smith in our claims department is the real expert in this area. Let me transfer you directly to her. In case we get disconnected, her extension is 431."*

When you contact the person who will handle the problem, be sure to explain it thoroughly. That spares the caller the hassle of telling it all over again, and perhaps growing even angrier.

Escalating the problem caller

Every once in a while, no matter how good you are at customer service, some calls will need to be escalated (forwarded) to a supervisor. Do not feel as though you have not done a good job; there are just some people who cannot be satisfied no matter what you say or do. You will please most of the customers most of the time, and that is pretty good.

IRATE CALLERS

1. What two components are part of effectively handling irate calls?

   _____

   _____

2. Why shouldn't you take the caller's hostility personally?

   _____

   _____

3. How can you get off on the right foot when talking to an irate caller?

   _____

   _____

4. Name the four basic steps to take when handling the irate caller.

   _____

   _____

5. When can you use an excuse?

   _____

   _____

6. How can a call transfer be managed efficiently?

   _____

   _____

I.Q. Test

Circle the letter for the right answer to these questions.

1. How long do you get to make a good first impression on the telephone?

    a. 4–6 seconds

    b. 30–45 seconds

    c. 1–4 minutes

2. What are buffer words?

    a. Words that add polish to your conversation

    b. Words that have no specific meaning

    c. First words of greeting used in answering a phone call

3. What percent of business calls get completed on the first try?

    a. 74 percent

    b. 43 percent

    c. 25 percent

4. When is a smile most important when handling a telephone call?

    a. When you greet the caller

    b. When you state your company name

    c. Before you pick up the phone

5. When is the customer right?

    a. When the complaint is legitimate

    b. Always

    c. Whenever he or she thinks so

6. When is it okay to hang up on a caller?

    a. When he or she is rude

    b. When you know you don't want the caller's business

    c. Never

7. When can you hear a smile?

    a. Never

    b. Always

    c. On your birthday

8. When should you offer help on the phone?

    a. Only when it's about your department

    b. Always

    c. Only if you have time to service the call

9. When is it okay to lie to a caller?

    a. Never

    b. When your boss tells you to

    c. When you don't know the answer

10. If you call a client and get voicemail, you should

    a. Hang up immediately

    b. Leave your name, then hang up

    c. Give your name, phone number, and a detailed message of why you're calling

I.Q. Answers

Here are the correct answers.

1. **a. 4–6 seconds.** The first indication of a company's excellence is how the phone is answered. It's entirely possible to "turn off" a prospective customer merely by answering the phone tardily, or in a rude or unfriendly fashion.

2. **c. First words of greeting used in answering a phone call.** Buffer words set up the most important part of any conversation, and are particularly effective when the phone is first answered. Use "Good morning," or "Thanks for calling," before you state your company or department name. Using a friendly buffer makes the caller feel welcome.

3. **c. 25%.** Find out the best times to reach the person. Make sure to leave a complete message if he or she is unavailable, or use voicemail to leave a personal message.

4. **c. Before you pick up the phone.** Don't wait to be friendly until you realize it's an important caller on the line—oftentimes that's too late. If you smile *before* you pick up the phone, you can be sure every caller will get the same warm welcome.

5. **c. Whenever he or she thinks so.** Perception is everything. Customers always think they're right. You'll never win an argument with a customer.

6. **c. Never.** If you're having difficulty with a caller, ask if he or she is able to hold and get some assistance. Remember, when you hang up on a person, you label yourself as rude.

7. **b. Always.**

8. **b. Always offer to assist the caller.** Even if you're not personally able to assist, you can always give the name and the telephone number of the person who can help.

9. **a. Never.** There is never a situation when lying to a caller is appropriate.

10. **c. Give your name, phone number, and a detailed message of why you're calling.** If possible, state a deadline for when you need a return call. Also, don't forget that most voicemail systems default to an operator. If you prefer, press "0" and see if someone else can help you.

"I'm Sorry"

Starting a sentence with "I'm sorry, Ms. Abraham is out of the office" is unnecessary. Use "I'm sorry" *only* when there is responsibility on your part. It is not your fault when someone is out of the office. Keep "I'm sorry" from becoming a universal excuse.

It is much more professional, helpful, and positive to say, *"Ms. Abraham is out of the office until Tuesday."* Then reintroduce yourself and make your Service Statement (see the sections on "Message Taking").

When a product or service hasn't been delivered, or you step on someone's toes, that's the right time to say, *"I'm sorry that happened,"* and, of course, to make amends immediately.

It's okay to say you're sorry when you step on someone's toes. But you don't need to be sorry when someone is away from the office or is in a meeting.

"Just a Second"

SEE ALSO "FIVE FORBIDDEN PHRASES"

"Just a second, I'll be right back." If you have ever said that to a caller, you have lied—not a big lie, but nevertheless an unnecessary lie. Why not tell the truth? You can say, *"It may take me a few minutes to get that information. Are you able to hold while I check on that for you?"* This is a real crowd-pleaser and lessens the pain and frustration of being put on hold. Once a caller knows why he or she is holding, he or she is much more willing to accommodate you.

Be sure to give a "visual" clue by telling the caller where you are going or what you are doing so he or she can experience the situation with you. It creates credibility.

"JUST A SECOND"

1. How many times have you been told "just a second," and more than two minutes elapsed? How did you feel?

   _____

   _____

2. What would you do if the caller is calling long distance or is unable to hold?

   _____

   _____

K.I.S.S. Method

The K.I.S.S. method stands for Keep It Simple, Simon.

As mentioned in the Introduction, this book is to show you how to be *friendlier to people*. This is *not* difficult. It just takes a little time and training–and, of course, observation of the Golden Rule: "Do unto others as you would have them do unto you."

Leave a Good Last Impression

You hear so much about making a good *first* impression–and that is certainly important. However, do not forget that leaving a good *last* impression is every bit as important.

Closing a call with "Uh-huh…uh-huh…okay, bye" leaves a caller with the feeling of casual dismissal–that he or she was not important to you and you were not interested in the call. The caller is left disappointed and annoyed.

Instead, try to include some of the conversation in your closing remarks. For instance: "Yes, I understand. I'll tell Joe and he'll take care of it. He's very good. And we do appreciate your call, Mr. Smith. Thanks for calling. It was good to talk with you. Goodbye." A remark like that leaves a great last impression!

Here are some other effective phrases to use in closing a phone conversation:

> *"Thanks for calling."*
>
> *"Please call again."*
>
> *"We appreciate your call."*
>
> *"Good talking to you."*

Do not just let a conversation die. Use your personality to express appreciation for being able to serve the caller. It is an important way to ensure that he or she will *want* to call back.

MNO 6 Message Mangling

During an average day, people frequently aren't available to take calls. Now with voicemail you often have a choice between leaving a recorded message or leaving it with a person. (Voicemail is covered later in this book.) Taking a message can become such a routine task that you might take messages without thinking about them. Or, because you are rushed, the original message might get shortened to a few words or phrases without many "social graces." Unfortunately, the called party may not get the meaning of the original message, and you might be accused of "message mangling." For instance:

> **Receptionist:** *"John's not here now. Want to leave a message?"*
>
> **Tim:** *"Yes, I sure do. I'd like to attend the meeting, but I'm unable to. I'm at the hospital; my wife is having a baby. I'll call him tomorrow."*

The message-taker hurriedly writes, "Unable to attend meeting. Will call."

What happens when John reads this message? He gets angry. "What does Tim mean he cannot attend? There is no good reason he cannot be there. We planned this meeting last month!"

Tim's actual message explained why he was unable to attend the meeting—a justified, self-explanatory reason. Had John gotten the complete story, he would have understood. Because the message taker was not thorough, the message received was not the message delivered. The message was mangled!

Miscommunication frequently occurs in the business world because of poor message taking. Word-for-word messages are important. In fact, messages should be read back to the caller. That is one reliable way to ensure that the message is what the caller wanted to say! It puts an end to message mangling, especially if you need to abbreviate the message.

Repeat the phone number in pairs of twos, such as: "291-ten-twelve." This lets the caller know you have got it correct.

When you take a message on the telephone,
be sure to include the date and time,
along with all other necessary information.
Messages without a date and time
have less impact on the person called.

MESSAGE MANGLING

1. Why are messages often mangled?

_____

_____

2. Why is the date and time important when taking a message?

_____

_____

3. Why does repeating a telephone number in pairs of twos help?

_____

_____

Message Taking #1

Why is "Can I take a message?" weak and ineffective? Because the response is all too often "No, that's okay, I'll call back." And how do you know the caller will? What if he or she needs information right then and there, or needs to order something immediately? You cannot be sure that this customer won't call a competitor next, all because of that weak little, "Can I take a message?" The cure is basic, but important: Instead of offering to *take* a message, offer to *help*. Be supportive, be proactive, and create credibility.

An example: *"Mr. Park is in a production meeting until 2:00 P.M. This is Mary. I'm his assistant. How can I help you? What can I do for you?"* The last two questions are key phrases.

This procedure is much more effective than an apathetic "Can I take a message?" or even "May I take a message?" When you use the "How can I help you?" offer, your *Service Statement* reaches out to the caller!

The Service Statement accomplishes four things:

1. You have placed Mr. Park somewhere—perhaps in a meeting or at lunch or at a sales conference. That's very important. The caller likes to know why he cannot reach the person he is calling. More important, though, is when he will return.

2. You have reintroduced yourself. Even if you've said your name in your initial greeting, once you've spoken past that, your name is usually erased from the caller's mind.

3. You've told the caller your relationship to the called party.

4. You've used the Service Statement for message-taking: "How can I help you? What can I do for you?" This is not so much to help the caller as much as it is to help the person you are taking the call for. This way, you will have much more of a message to deliver.

Use this message-taking process, and you'll be impressed with how many actual messages you'll write down, and how few of the "Oh well, I'll call back" responses you get. The messages you take will be more meaningful and will translate into greater customer satisfaction and future sales opportunities.

Every time you're able to help a caller beyond merely taking a message, you make a good mark for your company, your department, and yourself. You've been able to serve! And that's exactly what every phone call should be—an occasion for service.

MESSAGE TAKING #1

1. Why is "Can I take a message?" weak and ineffective?

_____

_____

2. How can you offer to help when taking a message?

_____

_____

3. Why does the proactive form of message taking translate into better customer service and sales opportunities?

_____

_____

Message Taking #2

Picture this: It's 8:30 A.M. You are at a customer's office, pitching hard to keep his business. The pressure is on and you could be out of the office all day.

While you are with your customer, the following scene is taking place at your office: Steve, your assistant, is busily preparing a new business proposal. At 9:05 A.M., the phone rings. The call is for you and Steve says, "She's not in, can I take a message?"

The caller replies, "No, that's okay, I'll call back." Steve, in his nicest voice, says, "Okay, fine, thank you," and hangs up.

Imagine that happening all day long, with all of your incoming calls. Think about Steve's reply. Now it is 4:00 P.M. and you're back at your office. You say to Steve, "Hi, any messages?" Steve says, "Nope, no messages."

But Steve is wrong. He should have had a whole *stack* of messages for you. Those calls could have been prospects for you, and they may have already called your competitors. The commonly-used statement "She's not in, can I take a message?" can cost a firm thousands of dollars in business. This questions invites the caller to slip out the back door by allowing him or her to respond, "No, I'll call back later."

Chances are there are three or four people in an office who can handle a particular incoming call, or can at least get the ball rolling. Customers are looking for a calm, confident voice to help them. No matter who initially answers the call, that person should assume 100% responsibility for handling that call professionally. To a caller who has never seen or done business with your company, the person answering the call *is* the company. That critical first impression can make or break the beginning of a business relationship.

If someone is taking time to call you, much more is needed than the ineffective "Can I take a message?" Here is what Steve should do and say:

Steve Should Do This	*Steve Should Say This*
Tell caller where	"Ms. Jones is out of the office…"
Tell caller when	"…until 4:00 P.M."
Tell caller who you are	"This is Steve."
Tell caller what you do	"I work with Ms. Jones."
Give caller the Service Statement	"How can I help you? What can I do for you?"

How and *what* are the key words. They signal open-ended questions that encourage the caller to talk.

If there is time, a front line person or assistant might also ask, "If you're able to share a little bit of the nature of your call with me, I can get the ball rolling for you." Sometimes, busy operators cannot afford to give substantial personal attention to a call. There are, however, effective alternatives. See "Message Taking."

MESSAGE TAKING #2

1. How can the phrase "He's not in, can I take a message?" cost a firm thousands of dollars worth of business?

   _____

   _____

2. In message-taking, name two "shoulds" that encourage the caller to talk.

   _____

   _____

Mirror on Your Desk

SEE ALSO "SMILE"

℞

All Telephone Doctor® employees have mirrors on their desks. It reminds them to smile before they pick up the phone whether the call is inbound or outbound. Do you have a mirror on your desk? You should. Callers can hear your smile.
You are welcome to call and order your mirrors from the Telephone Doctor®. They are fun to have, and a great reminder to SMILE.

Music (or Announcements) on Hold

"Hold music" can be a benefit or a detriment, depending on who is listening. If your company uses hold music and you are getting a lot of complaints, consider not using it.

Taped announcements are another choice for callers on hold. If you use this to tactfully promote your business and your product, it is certainly proactive, and often a help to your callers if you have specials or technical information. But remember, except when you need to go get more information, callers should never be put on hold for a substantial length of time.

Announcements have value only if they are of benefit to the caller—if you have unusual hours, specials, or upcoming events specials. For instance, if yours is an automotive shop, your announcement could explain the benefit of a better-treaded tire, or why a retreaded tire is of value. If yours is a flower shop, you could provide recorded plant-care tips. The possibilities are endless.

Never apologize for the hold during an announcement, and never tell the caller, "Your call is very important to us." The feeling here is: "If I'm so important to you, then why aren't you here to help me?"

Keep your announcements short, sweet, and of value to the caller. One more point: The person recording the hold message should be a professional who knows how to deliver an announcement. It needs to be recorded in a professional, upbeat manner, one that the caller will want to listen to. Monotones are out.

MNO 6 "No" at the Start of a Sentence

SEE ALSO "FIVE FORBIDDEN PHRASES"

The word *"no"* at the start of a sentence is unproductive, conveys rejection, and is too blunt. Sentences can be grammatically correct without the word *"no."* But this is not as easy as it sounds. Turn to the person next to you and ask, "Have you ever been to China?" He or she will probably say, "No, I haven't." But it would be just as correct to answer, "I haven't been there yet." That is much more pleasing to the ear.

If you think before you speak, you can turn every answer to a caller into a positive response. Simply eliminate the word "no" at the start of the sentence. Start the sentence with the next word. Or, better yet, start your sentence with the word you have just heard from the caller.

What kinds of answers about your company and its business could be improved by using this technique? Here is an example:

Caller: *"Can I get delivery today?"*

You: *"I wish we could. The truck has already left for the day. We can get it for you tomorrow."*

6
MNO

*O*bscene Phone Calls

During a recent Telephone Doctor® seminar, how to handle obscene phone calls came up. One of the ladies in the audience, an operator at a very busy company, raised her hand and said, "I just read them the Bible and they never call back."

Almost everyone at one time or another has received some sort of obscene phone call. They are not terribly easy to handle, whether you are at work or at home. Here are ways to manage them. Perhaps you can think of a few of your own.

1. Change your phone number or get an unlisted number. This is drastic, but it is real action that works.

2. Ask the phone company to put a tap on your phone to try to locate the perpetrator.

3. Keep a whistle by your phone. When you realize you have received a call that offends you, simply blow the whistle into the handset. It is painful for the caller, and it works!

4. Here is the recommended Telephone Doctor® technique that has been suggested by police departments: As soon as you hear obscenities, gently (that is the key word, gently) hang up the phone or disconnect. *Do not attempt to engage in dialog with a caller who is using obscene language.*

Customers who are very angry and using language offensive to you are handled differently. See "Irate Callers."

Here is some good news: With caller ID and call blocking services available from the phone company in most communities, the incidence of obscene phone calls has been decreasing.

Obscene Phone Calls

1. What are four techniques to handle obscene phone calls?

    _____

    _____

2. Name a basic rule for ending an obscene phone call:

    _____

    _____

People Before Paperwork!

SEE ALSO "SIX CARDINAL RULES OF CUSTOMER SERVICE"

Have you ever tried to talk on the phone with someone who was obviously doing something else during your conversation? Perhaps the person is going through papers, adding figures on a calculator, or finishing a note or memo—anything but paying attention to you. Maybe you can actually hear the computer keyboard being worked. The person talks in a distracted fashion, or worse, he or she asks you to wait while completing other tasks!

Let paper wait, not your people!

When you pick up the phone, stop what you are doing. Put your paperwork aside. It will not disappear, but your caller might! Type or do other tasks only when it pertains to the call. Acknowledge your callers. Let them know that they come first. (They really do!)

Remember: People before paperwork.

"Please…Thank You…You're Welcome"

SEE ALSO "SIX CARDINAL RULES OF CUSTOMER SERVICE"

"There ya go" is not "Thank you." "Uh-huh" is not "You're welcome."

If someone were to count, starting today, for one day, how many times you say "please," "thank you," and "you're welcome" to your callers, what do you think would be the total number? When a customer has spent money, he or she wants to hear: "Thank you. We appreciate your business." And when the *customer* takes the time to say, "Thank you," he or she does not want to hear a mumbled "Uh-huh." "You're welcome" is a pleasant phrase; use it often and don't be a mumbler. Remember to say, "Thank you" and "You're welcome."

Public Sector

Those who work in the public sector—in government, public utilities, or other "noncompetitive" agencies and organizations—have a tendency to believe they do not have a compelling need to serve their callers effectively. (After all, they're not Corporate America; they're the "only game in town"!) In reality however, nothing could be further from the truth.

Today, the expectations of taxpayers and utility customers are greater than ever before. Elections, bond issues, public service commission hearings, and so on are barometers of "customer service" quality in the public sector. Serving the requirements of customers who have urgent questions and need information, or have important complaints, is every bit as important in government as it is in the business community. Public sector employees, as well as private sector employees, need to be concerned with giving good customer service.

If you work in the public sector, how effectively you handle incoming calls is a key to improving the image of your agency. It is important that you understand how to serve callers in order to play a positive role in customer service. Today, simply having a telephone on your desk gives you enormous customer-service opportunities!

All the skills, concepts, and suggestions you will read in this book for improving telephone techniques apply equally to both public and private arenas. Good telephone manners are critically important to all of us!

66

PUBLIC SECTOR

1. If it is true that governments and utilities have no competition, why is it important for them to be nice?

_____

_____

2. Why is effective call-handling important to the image of the public sector?

_____

_____

3. Do techniques for improving telephone skills apply to the public sector as well as to the private sector?

_____

_____

Quality Is a Four-Letter Word

PQR 7

You hear so much today about "quality this" and "quality that." But instead of looking at "quality" as frosting on the cake, look at it as something you bake *into* the cake, a basic ingredient.

Quality comes from a four-letter word, and that word is *LOVE*.

There are different types of love. There is the love you have for your mother. You also may love music or a favorite hobby. And there is the love you have for your mate or significant other. Still another kind of love is the love of your job. And people who are out of a job often say, "I'd love to get a job."

There are 24 hours in a day, seven days in a week. Multiply 24 hours by seven days and you get 168 hours. Of the 168 hours in a week, most people work 40 hours. That is one-quarter of your week—23.8% of your week, to be exact—which goes for working. And that 23.8% provides you with 100% of your pay for all 168 hours.

If you are like most folks, everything you pay for—your mortgage or rent, your family's food, gasoline for your car, breakfast, lunch, dinner, snacks, a movie or a concert—is bought with the money from your paycheck, which comes from your job. Think about it. You almost have to be an ingrate not to appreciate your job.

If you love your job, quality customer service will follow. For the sake of your paycheck and your job, remember: Quality is a four-letter word. LOVE.

QUALITY IS A FOUR-LETTER WORD

1. Why shouldn't you consider quality as "frosting on the cake"?

_____

_____

2. Why is a job important to your well-being?

_____

_____

3. When you love your job, why is quality customer service automatic?

_____

_____

Receptionist

SEE ALSO "FRONT-LINE OPERATORS"

A receptionist is an important ambassador or representative of a company. As a receptionist, you have much more credibility and influence than you may realize. Concentrate on being positive, professional, and pleasant, and you will always be proud of what you do—and that will tell your customers that your company's services or products are worth consideration.

Returning Phone Calls

Not returning a phone call is like not using your turn signal: just plain rude. Even if you get too many calls to return each one yourself, you should *always* make sure that they get returned on your behalf by someone in your office.

The hardest calls to return are those of an unhappy customer or client. The Telephone Doctor® suggests you look at returning unhappy calls as the proverbial "second chance." In this situation, the customer is letting you know something is wrong and would like you to fix it. It is when the customer *is not* leaving angry messages that you need to be concerned—that is when he or she is taking the business somewhere else. One warning: Be careful when you say, *"I'll call you back by 5 o'clock"* (or whenever) on your message. There may be things that prevent you from returning these calls when you say you will, and then you have not lived up to your promise. Give yourself some breathing time when you promise a call back.

Rushing Callers
SEE ALSO "SIX CARDINAL RULES OF CUSTOMER SERVICE"

Always take time with callers;
rushing threatens them!

Face it: Most phone calls you receive are an interruption. Chances are, you do not get much chance to sit around and wait for the phone to ring. Therefore, when you answer a phone call, you may accidentally rush the caller because *you* are busy. This can be frustrating or annoying to the caller.

Give your full attention to the caller. Avoid giving quick, short, rushed answers, which are also intimidating. Unless it pertains to the conversation 100%, do not write, type, or talk to anyone else besides the caller. If you are going to write or type as you talk with someone, tell the caller that is what you are doing. If you do not, there tends to be too much silence and one of you will think the other isn't listening.

Here are a few quick, short answers that make people feel rushed. Try not to use them:

"Okay"

"Sure"

"Yes"

"Yeah"

"Uh-huh"

"No"

RUSHING CALLERS

1. What other short answers can you think of? List them here:

_____

_____

2. Write down some other, more helpful short answers that assure the caller you are listening. (Keep this list by your phone.)

_____

_____

Screening Calls

Screening, at best, is intimidating for the caller; at worst, screening is humiliating. There are three types of screens: a single, a double, and a triple. Here are examples:

1. **Single Screen:** *"Who's calling?"*

2. **Double Screen:** *"Who's calling, and what company are you with?"*

3. **Triple Screen:** *"Who's calling? What company are you with? What's this in reference to?"* (The person screening might as well be wearing a helmet and holding a rifle. It sounds like he or she is interrogating a prisoner!)

You may have been instructed to use the following call-screening questions: "Can I ask who's calling?" or "May I tell him/her who's calling?" Even these screens, however, can still offend the caller, because you are putting him or her through a procedure that may feel threatening.

Telephone Doctor®'s recommended, improved screening process is simple. It is a *two-step process* and involves the person doing the screening as well as the person for whom you're screening. If you are asked to screen telephone calls you will need to share this technique with that person.

Scenario 1

Caller: *"Mr. Lark, please."*

You: *"Thank you. I'll ring his office. Let me tell him who's calling, please."*

First, it is important to let the caller know *in advance* if the called party is there or not. Never screen the call and *then* tell the caller the party is not available. Second, the "Let me" technique is far less offensive than "Can I" or "May I tell him who's calling?"

Let's continue:

Caller: *"Yes, it's Rebecca Smith."*

You: *"Thanks, Ms. Smith. I'll ring his office."*
(Always use the caller's name after the screen.)

Then ring Mr. Lark, or otherwise let him know that Ms. Smith is on the line.

Now, Mr. Lark *must pick up the call using the caller's name.* There is little value to screening a call if the person called picks up the phone with just "Hello?" If you subject the caller to the screening scenario, make sure you use the information. Screen for identification, *not* elimination! Screen to *personalize* the telephone call.

Scenario 2

Caller: *"Is Irene in?"*

You: *"Yes. I'll ring her office. Let me tell her who's calling, please."*

or

You: *"Irene isn't in the office now; she'll be back at 3:00 P.M. My name is Chris. I'm her assistant; how can I help you? What can I do for you?"*

This screening method has several advantages. It creates credibility and redirects the conversation, and the caller still gets helped.

Here is another screening situation to be prepared for: Suppose you take a call, screen it, get the caller's name, and tell the boss who it is. Then you hear: *"Tell 'em I'm not here."* What do you do with calls the boss doesn't want to take? Especially after you screened them? In this less-than-perfect world, you need a technique for managing this situation.

There is a better technique than lying. You would not get hired if, in the interview, you said with a smile, "Yes, I'm Sue, and I'm an excellent liar." Here is a technique *instead of lying* that will make you look and feel good. Tell the caller, *"Mr. Lark, Ms. Francis is unavailable. My name is Chris. I'm her secretary* (or assistant, whatever title you have). *How can I help you? What can I do for you?"*

What you have done here is take control of the conversation and offer a truthful diversion. You have taken responsibility for the call, and by using the Service Statement, you are a hero!

74

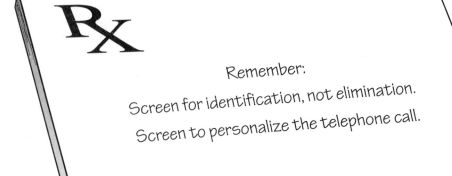

Remember:
Screen for identification, not elimination.
Screen to personalize the telephone call.

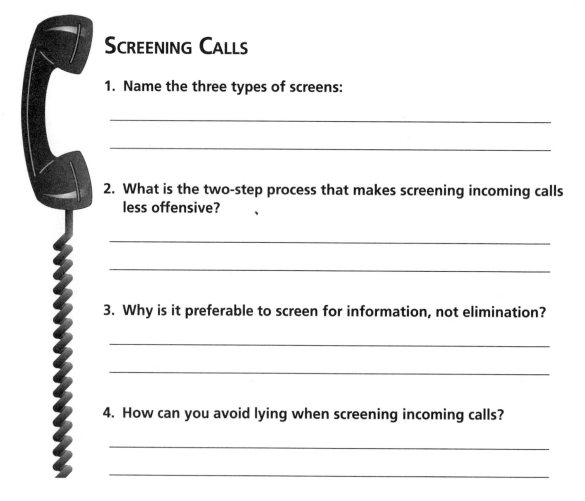

SCREENING CALLS

1. Name the three types of screens:

_____

_____

2. What is the two-step process that makes screening incoming calls less offensive?

_____

_____

3. Why is it preferable to screen for information, not elimination?

_____

_____

4. How can you avoid lying when screening incoming calls?

_____

_____

Getting past the screen

Wouldn't it be wonderful if every caller identified him- or herself right away? You would never have to screen a call again! Unfortunately, that is not the way things work most of the time. So when you make a telephone call, here's the recommended Telephone Doctor® method. Use it, and you will not get screened. There are three statements you need to make when you make the call:

1. *"This is Jordan Smith…"*

2. *"with XYZ Company in St. Louis, Missouri."*

3. *"I need to speak with Gerry Sparks."*

As a caller, when you give this full-disclosure statement at the beginning of the call, you will seldom get screened. You have done most of the work for the person answering the phone. You will get helped because you have been helpful.

Sometimes the person taking the call will still ask, even after you have delivered the full disclosure statement, "And what is this in regard to?" Take a one- or two-second theatrical pause, and say simply, "I'm interested in doing business with your company." It will get you through almost every time.

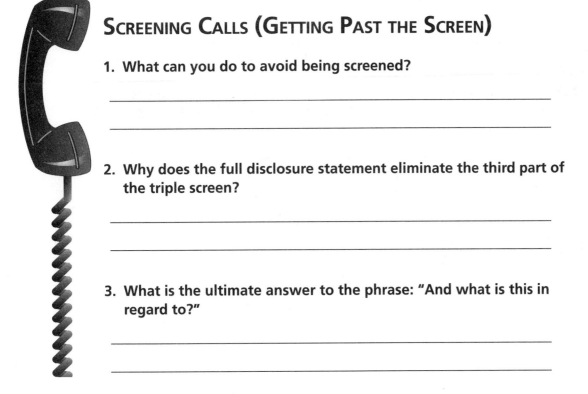

SCREENING CALLS (GETTING PAST THE SCREEN)

1. What can you do to avoid being screened?

_____

_____

2. Why does the full disclosure statement eliminate the third part of the triple screen?

_____

_____

3. What is the ultimate answer to the phrase: "And what is this in regard to?"

_____

_____

Six Cardinal Rules of Customer Service

Be sure to read these sections:

➤ **Be Friendly Before You Know Who It Is**

➤ **Company Jargon**

➤ **Don't Be Too Busy to Be Nice**

➤ **People Before Paperwork!**

➤ **"Please…Thank You…You're Welcome"**

➤ **Rushing Callers**

Slow Talkers

Slow talkers, like fast talkers, can be frustrating. Here is a technique that works wonders with a slow talker when he or she is stumbling and stammering, trying to ask for what he or she needs.

> **Caller:** *"Yes, I'm, uh, looking for…um, um, I ah…"*

> **You interject:** *"Are you calling for Abby, Drew, or Dana?"*

This is called the multiple-choice technique. You simply prompt the caller with three or four choices to help him or her decided what he or she might need. Here is another example:

> **You:** *"Did you need to change or add to your order?"*
> The caller will fill in the blanks for you.

Don't give up on slow talkers; just have a little more patience with them.

Smile

Perhaps at a seminar or presentation on telephone skills, you have been told, "You need to smile when you are on the telephone." Actually that is only half right. It is even better to smile *before* you pick up the telephone! If you are not friendly before you know who it is, afterward may be too late. Can you "hear" a smile? Of course you can. You will find it is difficult to be rude when you are smiling. It clearly changes the tone of your voice.

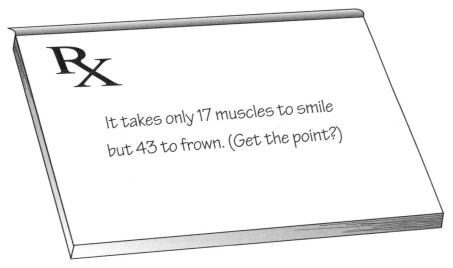

R/

It takes only 17 muscles to smile but 43 to frown. (Get the point?)

SMILE

1. When is the best time to smile when answering a call?

_____

_____

2. Why do you suppose that you can "hear" a smile?

_____

_____

3. What's the value of a mirror on the desk?

_____

_____

Speakerphones

Speakerphones should not be used during initial greetings on incoming or outgoing phone conversations. Do not use a speakerphone until you have asked for permission. Try this:

> *"Excuse me, Ms. Martin. I need to get up and look for some files while we're talking. Do you mind if I put you on the speakerphone?"*

That is the courteous thing to do. When somebody talks on a speakerphone without asking permission, the person on the other end of the call may infer that someone else is listening in. So don't initiate a conversation over a speakerphone.

And how do you get someone *off* a speakerphone? The quality of a conversation on a speakerphone is often intermittent. Tell the truth. Try this technique; it usually works:

> *"Excuse me, Ms. Martin, I'm having a difficult time* (hearing or) *understanding you. If you're able to pick up the receiver, I'd appreciate it."*

Speakerphones do have value; for example, at conference meetings. When they are used in this way, the participants need to follow some simple ground rules. If there are more than two people in the room with the speakerphone, each person should identify him- or herself before speaking. And when working with a group, you should identify to whom you are directing your question or comment.

Another fine use of a speakerphone is this: If you are on hold waiting for someone, put the call on your speakerphone. With your hands free, you can do other jobs at your desk–answering or reading memos, opening your mail, and so forth. When your party comes on the line, start out by saying, "Just a moment, let me take you off the speakerphone." Then go ahead with your conversation. This lets you put your time spent on hold to a productive use.

Try never to end a call while on a speakerphone. Always pick up the receiver at the end of the call and make a more personal closure to the conversation.

SPEAKERPHONES

1. When should you never use speakerphones?

_____

_____

2. What are the ground rules for using speakerphones?

_____

_____

3. When is the best time for using a speakerphone?

_____

_____

Swear-Stoppers

SEE ALSO "IRATE CALLERS"

It is no fun to have someone yell at you, let alone have someone swear at you. And it is not right, either. Unfortunately, there are people who have not learned that yet. You need to learn how to deal with them.

POINT #1: Never argue with such callers. Do not get into the ring with them. Don't go one round. You will lose every time.

POINT #2: When a caller starts to use abusive, foul language, interject—yes, with a smile; that is going to be the key—this swear-stopper: "Excuse me, I can handle your problem, but I cannot handle your abusive language."

Most people do not realize they are swearing. When you bring it to their attention in an unthreatening manner, it is much easier for them to take. Nine times out of 10, they will apologize for swearing and tell you how frustrated they are with the situation.

This is the perfect time to use the ASAP technique shown in "Irate Caller."

Rx

Remember the old adage, "You get more flies with sugar than you do with vinegar."

Three-Part Greeting

When you answer a telephone call, the first four to six seconds are critical because that is all the time you get to make a good first impression on the telephone. As basic and simple as that sounds, if the initial greeting in a phone call is ineffective, the opportunity to create immediate goodwill for a business is lost.

To create a good impression when initially greeting a caller, try this three-part approach:

1 The Buffer

That is the welcome mat that ushers the caller into your business. "Good morning," "Good afternoon,"—any words that tell the caller: "I am so glad you called," and "Thanks for calling."

Without the buffer words, your company or department name might come across as curt, hard, and cold. Have you ever called a company and heard "—ank…" when what he or she really said was "First National Bank?" If the right phone button is not pushed in time, or the mouthpiece is not exactly at the person's mouth, part of the greeting can get cut off. It is not a disaster if buffer words get cut off, but your company and department name should never be. Buffer words set up the most important part of the greeting, which comes next: Your company or department name.

2 Company or Department Name

After the important buffer words, company or department names should be said confidently and clearly—never rushed, mumbled, or run together.

3 Your Name

Stating your name does two things: It speeds the rapport-building process, and 80% of the time, when you give your name, the caller will respond in kind with his or her name. If a caller has to ask, "Who's this?" or "Who am I speaking with?" it simply means you've answered the phone ineffectively. An ineffective initial greeting can result in lost business.

An expert initial greeting will create goodwill and start the conversation off on the right foot. Mix together the three parts of the recommended greeting and serve them with a big smile: *"Good morning, XYZ Company, this is Steve."* Then stop. (Remember, in the initial greeting, anything after your name erases your name. "How can I help you?" *is not necessary in the initial greeting.* It is not wrong, merely unnecessary. "How can I help you" is best used in message-taking situations.

82

For more information about the Service Statement "How can I help you?", see "Message Taking #1" and "Message Taking #2."

Rx Use the Telephone Doctor® "This Is" technique in your three-part greeting: "This is Betty." Do not say "Betty speaking." Betty Speaking is married to Bob Speaking. They have two children, Judy Speaking and Billy Speaking. People remember the last thing they hear, so let that be your name, not "speaking."

THREE-PART GREETING

1. Name the three parts of a greeting to a caller:

_____

_____

2. Why is the buffer important?

_____

_____

3. What does giving your name achieve?

_____

_____

Tone of Voice

In person, you are like a television set. You have sight, sound, color, and motion. On the telephone, you are like a radio. All you have is voice, tone of voice, and the listener's imagination.

The tone of your voice is especially important on the telephone, because it is the key indicator of your emotional state. In person, facial expressions and body language are part of the signals you send along with tone of voice. On the telephone, however, it is like listening to the radio: no visual signal. The tone of your voice assumes a greater role as a communication tool.

There are a number of ways you can change the meaning of a sentence, just by emphasizing one word or another. Example: "I won't be working today." This sentence can have a different meaning, depending on which of the five words you emphasize. Test this with tone of voice. Try reading this sentence aloud, adding in the following emotions or feelings:

Angry: *"I won't be working today."*

Bored: *"I won't be working today."*

Confident: *"I won't be working today."*

Happy and smiling: *"I won't be working today."*

Notice that the same words have different meanings with each tone of voice. So, once again, you need to remember: smile before you pick up the phone, and continue to smile while you talk on the phone. This welcomes the caller and sets the stage for positive, productive communication.

Transferring Calls

SEE ALSO "IRATE CALLERS"

R̲X

Transfer the problem along with the caller.
Do not just dump the call to someone else.
Let the person who will handle the problem
know what is coming.

STU 8 *U*navoidable Delays in Answering

Many companies have a policy that any inbound phone call should be answered no later than the third ring. But what happens when this is not possible—for instance, when you are busy or in the office alone?

When you have answered a phone that has rung more than the preferred three times, use this apology buffer:

> *"I'm sorry it rang so long. XYZ Company, this is Victoria."*

> or

> *"I'm sorry it rang so long. Mr. Lee's office, this is Jerry."*

This special greeting accomplishes two things:

➤ It provides an immediate apology.

➤ It immediately helps defuse the caller's frustration.

When you feel uncomfortable with the number of times the telephone has rung and it is your turn to answer it, let your buffer words be the apology, rather than ignoring the delay altogether. It does not make the situation right, but it does ease the pain. Without the apology buffer, the caller usually says (or at least thinks to him- or herself), "Where the heck were you? What took so long?" With the apology buffer, the objection can be stated beforehand.

UNAVOIDABLE DELAYS IN ANSWERING

1. What is more important than answering the phone within three rings?

    _____

    _____

2. Why is it important to have a special buffer for these unavoidable delays?

    _____

    _____

3. What does it accomplish?

    _____

    _____

Voicemail—Curse or Cure?

Believe it or not, there was a time when there was no voicemail, no automated attendant, no "I'm not at my desk right now. Please leave a message." It was just people answering phones and taking messages.

Now we have both. Are we better off with or without voicemail? Is it a curse or a cure? If your office has voicemail, or the places you call do, these guidelines and tips will be very helpful.

Voicemail was not invented or installed to replace operators or take care of customer service. Voicemail was intended to do two things:

➤ *To answer on the first ring, and*

➤ *To expedite the phone call*

Although voicemail does achieve both of these aims, it has been proven time and time again that what callers really want is to hear a friendly, personal voice on the other end of the line.

There are three parts of voicemail: your personal greeting, the automated attendant, and the messages you leave for others.

Your personal greeting

This is the part where you get to shine. The greeting that you put on your own voicemail box is extremely important. If you feel as though you are missing messages, it could be the way your greeting sounds to the caller. Simply put, your greeting needs to be great.

If you are using the standard "Hi, this is Bob. I'm either on the phone or away from my desk right now," you need to rethink your greeting. If your voicemail greets the caller, you are obviously on the phone or away from your desk. Use those very precious and few seconds to your best advantage. Be creative, and give pertinent information to the caller.

First of all, callers need and want to know the following:

1. To whom they are speaking, and what department they have reached.

2. Where you are (not where you are *not*)

3. When you will return

4. Who can they turn to for more information

5. Escape options (how they can exit the system or reach someone else)

An effective voicemail greeting reads like this:

"Hi, this is Nancy Friedman in the sales department. I'm in New York at a sales conference, and will be back in St. Louis on Monday, June 9th. If you need something right now, please call my assistant, Debbie, at Box 47, or zero out to the operator. Otherwise, go ahead and leave your name and phone number, twice and slow please, along with a message so I can get back to you. I do check my messages and return all calls or have them returned on my behalf. Thanks a lot, and make it a great day."

This greeting tells the caller who was reached, where the person is, and when that person will return. There are also two escapes for the caller, and an assurance that the call will be returned.

Here is another option. It advises the caller you will not be checking messages.

"Hi, this is Nancy Friedman in the sales department. I'm in New York at a sales conference, and will be back Monday, June 9th. I won't be calling in to check these messages, so if you need me, please call Debbie, my assistant, at voicemail box 47 and she'll find me. Again, I won't be checking messages until June 9th. Thanks for calling. Talk with you soon."

Letting the callers know whether you will be checking your voicemail is very informative. Give good, clear directions for the caller. Surveys report that most callers are prone to leaving a message when they hear that you do check your messages often.

Everyone knows that callers respond better to a friendly greeting than a robotic one, so be sure you're smiling when you record your greeting. And just how will you know if you are smiling? Two ways: One, record in front of a mirror, and two, call your own recording and listen to it. Be sure to audit it before you let it go out "over the air," so to speak.

Daily greetings

Should you record a new greeting every day? Simply put, anytime you use a day or date within a greeting you will need re-record the message. It is so sad to hear a "Happy New Year!" greeting in February, and it is also unprofessional. At holiday times, use your voicemail to wish callers the appropriate holiday. *Anytime* you use a time or date reference in your voicemail recording, be sure you re-record appropriately.

Some people complain that it takes too much time to rerecord a daily message, when actually it takes no more than 10 to 12 seconds. You should brush your teeth longer than that. Do not make such a big deal about it. Your voicemail greeting is very important. Don't shake it off as something that's not. It represents you, and *you* are very important.

It is a good idea to let your callers know if you're going to be out of the office longer than the day they called. Why? Because if your message simply tells the caller to "leave a message and you'll get back as soon as possible," you could miss a lot of opportunities. Salespeople will verify this—important sales have been lost because calls weren't returned "as soon as possible."

The automated attendant

This is affectionately labeled "the Groaner," (because most people just groan when they hear the lethargic "Thank you for calling XYZ Company. If you know your party's extension, please press it now, blah, blah, blah.") Instead of a friendly personal greeting, you hear a robotic delivery from a machine.

Since the automated attendant isn't universally appreciated by the public, you can reduce the number of groans by doing three things:

1. Replace the robotic voice with a friendly, personal message.

When people say they hate voicemail, they often really mean they hate the impersonal, robotic voice they have to deal with. That voice is the public's first contact with your company and it needs to be a friendly, positive experience. Remember, you are not married to the voice that comes with the equipment you have purchased. The most important part of the automated attendant is the friendly tone of the voice that your callers hear.

2. Tell callers how to reach a human being quickly.

It is helpful and appreciated if your attendant message lets the caller know—first thing—how to bypass the message and go directly to an operator. Most systems allow callers to "zero out" of the recorded greeting. Pressing "0" may allow callers to immediately select an extension or be connected with an operator.

3. Make sure the recorded greeting is friendly and positive.

If your answering machine or automated attendant tells the caller, "We're closed now," consider re-recording the message. It is much better to tell the caller when you *are* open than negative information about being closed. If yours is a small business, leave a tip or two or some piece of valuable information that the caller can take away with him or her.

When you leave a message for others

This is your opportunity to be great. Leaving a voicemail message is your electronic business card. You wouldn't give someone a business card that contained incorrect or outdated information, would you? Then why leave anything but a *great* voicemail message?

When someone goes to lunch, is gone for a few days and then comes back to the office, or checks in from the road, the voicemail system may say something like, "Hello, you have 32 new messages." If your message is somewhere in that mob, it better be great. Otherwise, like junk mail, it can get zapped real fast.

There are three kinds of voicemail messages: poor, average, and great. Here is a sample of each; you can decide which you would like to receive.

Poor: *"Hi, Nancy, this is Bob. Give me a call, please."*

Bob who? What if the recipient knows several people named Bob and does not recognize the voice?

Average: *"Hi, Nancy, this is Bob Smith, with Acme Vending. Please call me at 291-1012. I have something to ask you. Thanks."*

He left the company name. Big deal. But what did he want? Why did he waste a call to just say he had something to ask? Why didn't he leave the question?

Voicemail is perfect for one-way communication. Bob wasted both his and the recipient's time by just leaving a name and number. Including the question in his message would have helped the recipient prepare an answer before returning the call.

Great: *"Hi, Nancy, this is Bob Smith, at Acme Vending, calling to say hi and remind you that the proposal you wanted will be on your desk Friday. If we can meet Monday afternoon to go over the ideas, I can have the special order ready by the time you return from vacation. Please call me, or my secretary Susan, at 291-ten-thirteen and let me know what time I should be at your office on Monday the 29th. Enjoy your vacation and I look forward to seeing you. Thanks a lot. Again, Bob Smith at Acme, 291-ten-twelve."*

This great message has all the requirements necessary to do business, and the phone number was repeated! (Numbers left just once, and spoken too quickly, are a real irritant.) And don't forget to smile when you leave your message.

It seems like common sense to remind you to leave your message in an upbeat, personable and friendly fashion. However, from your own experience you know it is still not very common. Messages that are left in the friendly tone seem to get a quicker response.

There are techniques for leaving a voicemail message that will encourage someone to call you back. One is to use a specific callback time. *"I need to hear from you by 4 P.M. on Thursday, May 3rd."* Stated deadlines are much more effective than "Call me as soon as possible," or "Call me as soon as you can."

Most voicemail systems will allow you to play back what you recorded and offer an opportunity to re-record. Take advantage of that feature to listen to *what* you said, and *how* you said it. Replaying your message will help you ensure that you have left a friendly and complete message.

Do not leave bad news on a voicemail.
Leave a message that says you need to talk
with the person about an important matter.
Bad news should normally
not be conveyed through voicemail.

Voicemail General Tips

➤ Be prepared before picking up the phone. Expect your called party *not* to be available; have your voicemail message *planned* ahead of time. Stammering a confused and disorganized message sounds very unprofessional.

➤ Be friendly and *smile* when you are recording, both on your greeting and any messages you leave for others.

➤ *Talk* the message—do not sound as though you are reading it. Put your personality into it. Use contractions. Talk to the machine as though the person is standing right there looking at you.

➤ Request a specific callback time when necessary. Leave stated deadlines.

➤ Learn to use voicemail to your advantage. Remember that approximately two-thirds of business communications is one-way information.

➤ Do not dump callers into voicemail without first *asking* if they would like to be put into the system. Some callers may simply need to be redirected to someone who can help them directly; others may object to using voicemail.

VOICEMAIL

1. What is the advantage of recording your own greeting rather than using the script or voice that came with the system?

_____

_____

2. What information should be included in your greeting?

_____

_____

3. What are some of the advantages of an automated attendant?

_____

_____

VWX 9 | *W*e Are Customers to Each Other

Why is it that "inside calls" are often treated differently than "outside calls?" In many organizations, the type of ring indicates an inside call–for instance, short rings rather than long ones. These are sometimes answered with a brisk "Yeah?" But it makes good sense to answer the telephone the same way all the time. Callers from inside your company deserve the same professional treatment that you give to outside callers!

Customer service is a high priority with most companies, and this sense of good service must start from within. If high-quality service is not practiced within, it will probably not get out over the phone lines to customers and clients.

The three-part greeting you read about earlier is good for inside calls, too: *"Good morning, Accounting. This is Steve."*

Remember, we are customers to each other.

WE ARE CUSTOMERS TO EACH OTHER

1. **How should in-house calls be treated?**

   _____

   _____

2. **Why does customer service begin within an organization?**

   _____

   _____

"We Can't Do That"

SEE ALSO "FIVE FORBIDDEN PHRASES"

This phrase is guaranteed to get your customer's blood boiling. To many people, it is a challenge. Why challenge someone to seek a competitor who *can* "do that"? Try this instead: "That's a tough one. Let's see what we can do." Then find a solution.

There is no reason to ever repeat the negative. There is no need to remind the caller of what you *cannot* do. Much of the time, you'll find an acceptable positive alternative.

When you must, how do you let callers down gently? Use the "Wish" statement:

"Mr. Avery, I wish we could. That would be great. However, it's not an option. It's a great idea, though. What else can we think of?"

The "Wish" statement shows callers you have been listening, and that you agree (that is very important). Customers hear, "You are right." You have acknowledged their need or idea, yet told them you are not able to help them realize it. But you still did not say, "We can't do that." You would be amazed how frustrated customers get when you tell them, "We can't do that."

Welcome Guest

SEE ALSO "THREE-PART GREETING"

R_X

When your front doorbell rings,
and you open it to find an old friend,
you welcome him or her in, don't you?
Do the same thing with your
business callers—welcome them in.
Make every caller a welcome guest.

X-Rated

In Telephone Doctor® language, an x-rating brands a company as a place never to do business again. X-rated companies do not last long. By treating their customers with an uncaring attitude, these companies guarantee that customers will look elsewhere to get their hair cut, their printing done, or their cars repaired.

When clients are not treated properly, they go elsewhere. Do not make the mistake of encouraging an x-rated reputation for your company. That makes the competition a little stronger and your company a little weaker. So do everything you can to keep that from happening.

TRUE TELEPHONE TALES

A mother, shopping by phone for her daughter's wedding shower present, was looking for some fancy bathroom tissue with writing on it. She reached a store that might carry it. She introduced herself with, "Hi, my name is Julia. I'm trying to locate some unusual bathroom tissue paper. It has writing on it." The clerk replied very coldly, "We don't have any." In a second effort, the mother said with a big smile in her voice, "You know the kind I'm looking for—it says 'Happy Birthday' or 'Congratulations' or something fun on it." The clerk again bluntly repeated, "I said, we don't have any." And with that, the clerk branded his store as x-rated in the mind of the mother looking for a gift. Neither she nor her friends and associates whom she told about the experience would ever shop there again.

X-RATED

1. Name three businesses that have earned your x-rating.

_____

_____

2. What did they do that cost them your business?

_____

_____

3. How many people did you tell about the poor treatment you received?

_____

_____

4. Picking the worst of your three x-rated businesses, what should they have done differently? List at least two things.

_____

_____

"You'll Have to…"

SEE ALSO "FIVE FORBIDDEN PHRASES"

"You'll have to…"

Wrong. The only things the caller *has* to do are die and pay taxes. If you tell callers what they have to do, they often will not do it. People do not like to be ordered around. Instead, use phrases such as these:

"You'll need to…"

"Here's how we can help with that."

"The next time that happens, here's what you can do."

Remember, you take orders from your clients,
you do not give them.
You request; you do not demand.
Telling someone what he or she "needs"
to do is softer and less offensive.

Zest

The dictionary defines zest as "stimulating or exciting quality. Keen enjoyment; gusto"—for example: a zest for life.

This book started with A for Attitude. Now here we are at Z for Zest! We hope we have helped you improve your telephone skills and customer service abilities. The idea is for you to be very good at what you do—to have a zest for helping people.

It's fun to be good at your job. And that will help you have a zest for your job and your life.

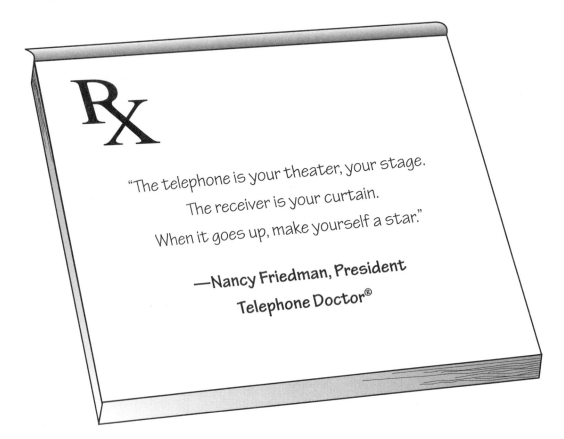

"The telephone is your theater, your stage.
The receiver is your curtain.
When it goes up, make yourself a star."

—Nancy Friedman, President
Telephone Doctor®

Now Available From

CRISP LEARNING

Books•Videos•CD-ROMs•Computer-Based Training Products

Subject Areas Include:

Management

Human Resources

Communication Skills

Personal Development

Marketing/Sales

Organizational Development

Customer Service/Quality

Computer Skills

Small Business and Entrepreneurship

Adult Literacy and Learning

Life Planning and Retirement

VER.D

CRISP WORLDWIDE DISTRIBUTION

English language books are distributed worldwide. Major international distributors include:

ASIA/PACIFIC

Australia/New Zealand: In Learning, PO Box 1051, Springwood QLD, Brisbane,
Australia 4127   Tel: 61-7-3-841-2286, Facsimile: 61-7-3-841-1580
ATTN: Messrs. Gordon

Philippines: National Book Store Inc., Quad Alpha Centrum Bldg, 125 Pioneer Street,
Mandaluyong, Metro Manila, Philippines   Tel: 632-631-8051, Facsimile: 632-631-5016

Singapore, Malaysia, Brunei, Indonesia: Times Book Shops. Direct sales HQ: STP Distributors, Pasir Panjang Distrientre, Block 1 #03-01A, Pasir Panjang Rd, Singapore
118480   Tel: 65-2767626, Facsimile: 65-2767119

Japan: Phoenix Associates Co., Ltd., Mizuho Bldng, 3-F, 2-12-2, Kami Osaki,
Shinagawa-Ku, Tokyo 141   Tel: 81-33-443-7231, Facsimile: 81-33-443-7640
ATTN: Mr. Peter Owans

CANADA

Crisp Learning Canada, 60 Briarwood Avenue, Mississauga, Ontario, Canada L5G
3N6 Tel: (905) 274-5678, Facsimile: (905) 278-2801
ATTN: Mr. Steve Connolly/Mr. Jerry McNabb

Trade Book Stores: Raincoast Books, 8680 Cambie Street, Vancouver, B.C., V6P 6M9
Tel: (604) 323-7100, Facsimile: (604) 323-2600   ATTN: Order Desk

EUROPEAN UNION

England: Flex Training, Ltd., 9-15 Hitchin Street, Baldock, Hertfordshire, SG7 6A,
England Tel: 44-1-46-289-6000, Facsimile: 44-1-46-289-2417
ATTN: Mr. David Willetts

INDIA

Multi-Media HRD, Pvt., Ltd., National House, Tulloch Road, Appolo Bunder, Bombay,
India 400-039   Tel: 91-22-204-2281, Facsimile: 91-22-283-6478
ATTN: Messrs. Aggarwal

SOUTH AMERICA

Mexico: Grupo Editorial Iberoamerica, Nebraska 199, Col. Napoles, 03810 Mexico, D.F.
Tel: 525-523-0994, Facsimile: 525-543-1173   ATTN: Señor Nicholas Grepe

SOUTH AFRICA

Alternative Books, PO Box 1345, Ferndale 2160, South Africa
Tel: 27-11-792-7730, Facsimile: 27-11-792-7787   ATTN: Mr. Vernon de Haas